I0889574

LORD, HEAR MY CRY

Lord, Hear My Cry

The Penitential Psalms for Lent

Victor M. Cancino, SJ

Paulist Press
New York / Mahwah, NJ

Scripture texts in this work are taken from the *New American Bible, revised edition* © 2010, 1991, 1986, 1970 Confraternity of Christian Doctrine, Washington, D.C. and are used by permission of the copyright owner. All Rights Reserved. No part of the New American Bible may be reproduced in any form without permission in writing from the copyright owner.

Cover image by serge shirshov/Shutterstock.com
Cover and book design by Lynn Else

Copyright © 2026 by Victor Manuel Cancino

All rights reserved. No part of this publication may be reproduced, stored in a retrieval system, or transmitted in any form or by any means, electronic, mechanical, photocopying, recording, scanning, or otherwise, without either the prior written permission of the Publisher, or authorization through payment of the appropriate per-copy fee to the Copyright Clearance Center, Inc., www.copyright.com. Requests to the Publisher for permission should be addressed to the Permissions Department, Paulist Press, permissions@paulistpress.com.

Library of Congress Cataloging-in-Publication Data
Names: Cancino, Victor M. author
Title: Lord, hear my cry: the Penitential psalms for Lent / Victor M. Cancino, SJ.
Description: Paperback. | New York: Paulist Press, [2026] | Summary: "A Lenten meditation based on the seven penitential psalms"— Provided by publisher.
Identifiers: LCCN 2025022800 (print) | LCCN 2025022801 (ebook) | ISBN 9780809157792 paperback | ISBN 9780809189472 ebook
Subjects: LCSH: Catholic Church—Prayers and devotions | Penitential Psalms—Meditations | Lent—Meditations | LCGFT: Meditations | Devotional literature | Prayers
Classification: LCC BX2170.L4 C35 2026 (print) | LCC BX2170.L4 (ebook) | DDC 242/.34—dc23/eng/20250924
LC record available at https://lccn.loc.gov/2025022800
LC ebook record available at https://lccn.loc.gov/2025022801

ISBN 978-0-8091-5779-2 (paperback)
ISBN 978-0-8091-8947-2 (ebook)

Published by Paulist Press
997 Macarthur Boulevard
Mahwah, NJ 07430
www.paulistpress.com

Printed and bound in the
United States of America

Dedicado a mis primeros maestros
de la fe, mi apa y ama,
en memoria de Santiago.

Contents

Preface

This Lenten guide highlights the seven psalms designated as "penitential": Psalms 6, 32, 38, 51, 102, 130, and 143. A number of psalms fit the category of "penitential," but only these seven have been grouped together and recognized as a category since the seventh century. During Lent they offer a meditation of their own, rooted in the theme of lament. In their piercing language, filled with anguish and longing for wholeness, you will find a tangible reflection from the psalmist on personal and collective guilt. And yet this is not the source of their power. The seven Penitential Psalms have a way of entering into the fragile aspects of human nature and somehow still managing to point to a hopeful horizon. When seen through the lens of faith, hope becomes their staying power.

How to use this Lenten reflection? The nine chapters that follow are my own contemplations after sitting with each of the Penitential Psalms. Rather than providing an exegetical commentary for each passage, I have kept the writing pastoral and sensitive to the way the powerful words of Scripture can shed light on realities like despair. If the reflections help your prayer, use them. If they do not help, leave them behind—a slow read of these seven psalms by themselves is enough for a good Lenten contemplation.

This book may be used during any season. Indeed, the journey of the soul has its own timing and its own hidden understanding that waits for the Lord. Place your hope in the word that comes to you.

One suggestion is to take one chapter a day during Lent as your own personal aid to prayer. Moving slowly through this work in this manner will create a novena—nine days of focused prayer through the nine chapters of this book.

May God's presence guide you on this pilgrimage of hope through the Penitential Psalms.

1

Lament

My earliest memory was a vision of angels—a vision that came to life through Mom. When I was five or six, she taught me how to pray with my imagination. I remember kneeling during the middle of Mass with Mom right beside me. She leaned over and whispered in my ear, "Pay attention—now is when you pray really hard. Now is when *diosito santo* comes down from heaven with all his angels around him." It was easy to let my imagination take over, to envision the invisible illuminated throughout Scripture.

The psalms repeatedly mention the name *Adonai Sabaoth*, Lord of Hosts. The sacred title suggests an image of God synonymous with all-encompassing awesome power, who solemnly enters a physical space surrounded majestically by angels. Every sung or recited *Sanctus* at Mass summons this image. Even as a child I seemed to understand that God and Mom somehow made up the center of my universe. I felt safe in that world.

A second early memory brings me back to church, this time in an empty sanctuary where Dad was kneeling in audible prayer, the kind that comes from a deep wound. He was crying out with loud sighs caused by unknown grief. His lament was tied to the human condition, a realization that each of us is limited and perhaps powerless to change the devastating situations we face. But we must walk through this crucible nonetheless. Without faith, this kind of grief can lead to despair. With faith, it can be a lamentation with the potential to heal one's emotional health and spirit. I sat a few pews behind Dad that day and silently wondered, Could not the all-encompassing, powerful God make right whatever dreadful situation Dad was carrying at this moment?

Do you not hear his cry, *Adonai Sabaoth*?

In the following reflections, I hope to take the reader on a journey into the human condition—a condition highlighted by fragility. Our companions on this pilgrimage are the seven Penitential Psalms found in Scripture. The turmoil discovered in these psalms is not unlike the dramatic internal prayer of my own parents. At times my parents were filled with hopeful expectation; at other times with piercing lament. I noticed that over the years, their prayers have been answered. It only took the practice of waiting.

Lament is powerful. It is a core feature found in the psalms, and one that will guide us through Lent.

2

Heal

Do not reprove me in your anger, LORD,
  nor punish me in your wrath.
Have pity on me, LORD, for I am weak;
  heal me, LORD, for my bones are
    shuddering.

Psalm 6:2–3

"Heal me." How much time does it take to utter this plea aloud from a place of honest depth? The spiritual journey would say that a lot of time in required. How about, give or take, forty days?

Lent is an ideal liturgical time to move into this space. Sometimes, as in the case of the first Penitential Psalm, the right time to make this prayer is at the eleventh hour. Addicts, people on their sickbed, those hitting rock bottom for a myriad of reasons, or (insert your own situation here) are sometimes forced to cry out from their fatigue and desperation. It is hard to find better words than the psalmist's: "Heal me, LORD." We discover that this particular psalmist is on his deathbed: "For my bones are shuddering." Shocking to some of us, there is no acknowledgment of sin in this passage. Instead, the realization is the discovery of limits. I am limited. I can hurt others—more often than I am willing to admit—and I can carry my own wounds for an unbearable length of time. Until, of course, I reach my limit.

These lessons come too often at a high cost. Why is it that a person of faith will come to a great test of that faith and be distracted from the condition of her soul and flesh? "My bones are shuddering." At the same time, every Lent we begin with Jesus's own test of faith in the desert. The Gospels suggest that Jesus *must* pass through this abandoned space, and every one of Jesus's followers since will take a similar path in life or death. "Take my yoke upon you, and learn from me" (Matt 11:29). My burden is light, says the Teacher. While Psalm 6 speaks of physical threats due to illness and potential enemies, there are also spiritual deaths through which one may pass. I have died many times in this way.

"Have pity on me, for I am weak." Have we all recovered from COVID-19 yet? Right before this global epidemic that changed our daily lives, I went through one of those spiritual deaths. But as the famous dog whisperer Cesar Millan once said, reflecting on the significance of *Día de los Muertos*, "Death is life." This gem of wisdom is what Psalm 6 hints at, without necessarily resolving anything—and it is something that would take me years to unravel.

"Heal me, LORD." For even in death there is life.

3

Fear

My soul too is shuddering greatly—
  and you, LORD, how long...?
Turn back, LORD, rescue my soul;
  save me because of your mercy.
For in death there is no remembrance of
    you.
  Who praises you in Sheol?

Psalm 6:4–6

One dominant feature of the psalms is the way a range of human emotions is exposed to the attentive hearer. While the voice in one psalm cries out with fear, another voice speaks with calm and wonder. So it happens that one voice questions being cut off from God in the land of the dead, called Sheol. Meanwhile, another voice reaches a great depth of intuition about the Creator's presence, one that may be found in the most unlikely of places: "If I ascend to the heavens, you are there; if I lie down in Sheol, there you are" (Ps 139:8).

A lingering awareness of fleeting time seems to cast a shadow over the present moment in the lament phase of this Penitential Psalm. The voice asked a reasonable question: "How long?" In my own history, I developed a sensitivity toward time as it offered a necessary space for the slow healing work of God. This was especially true when lament was present, as in the length of time it took to finally forgive my father over repeated attempts.

At its height, the COVID-19 epidemic would jolt much of the world out of normality. The crisis hit Italy, the place where I lived and studied for four years, with devastating force. Right before the global shift, my own life quickly unraveled in the spring of 2019.

The Salish of the Flathead Indian Reservation, where I currently live, will enter sweat lodges to unload their knapsacks—that is, any heavy burdens or things they have carried throughout the week. My knapsack was filled to the brim, and I did not know how to let things go. I could feel the things I had carried over time grow heavier. Does anyone know the right time to let go?

"How long?"

The church designates a liturgical season, Lent, when all the faithful are asked to let go of something. It becomes a time to practice the spiritual exercise of letting go, especially when we recognize that a limit has been reached.

My own limit came after I successfully finished a course of study in Sacred Scripture from a prestigious academic institute in Rome. I lived in the only

Jesuit community in the world where you needed to pass two qualifying language exams in order to move in and become an official member. Over the years, this requirement has softened. Today Jesuit students can move into the Biblicum while preparing for their Hebrew and Greek entrance exams. After three and a half years of study, I finished my coursework, along with my final thesis on comparisons between illustrious figures from the ancient world and the biblical world. Rather than take a victory lap around Europe, I was exhausted, tired of Rome, and ready to move on.

What I did not understand at the time was that my fatigue did not come from the Eternal City. I was tired of feeling stuck, confused, and divided within—in short, fearful.

"Turn back, LORD, rescue my soul."

Fear consists of several layers that merit sorting. Fear is healthy if we live in an area full of grizzly bears and rez (feral) dogs. It can make us keep a constant vigil. Fear can be paralyzing when the imagination of it lingers and follows us, a constant presence that we cannot shake. At these times we have to name it, but if nothing comes to mind, it is just fear. St. Augustine writes a lot about the topic. He describes fear as a potential starting point for the new convert. The neophyte to the faith would do well to imagine complete separation from the Creator. A life that remains separated from the source of love should bring a man or woman to a place of examination for the present situation of their life. Even St. Ignatius of Loyola believed that if someone sought to change their life around for the better, a good look at their sins and a desire for reconciliation was enough for redemption.

But we were never meant to live in a constant state of fear. I entered religious life for reasons both clear and hidden to me. The silent call from God rang loudly in my heart as an invitation to follow Christ unreservedly and completely. The hidden part of my decision to enter the novitiate was more complicated to grasp. I had a powerful sense of running away from a world I felt was filled with conflict. The church for me always represented a safe place, a space where I felt protected in the arms of a loving Father. How could I have known back then, at the age of twenty-one, that life within the church was not divorced from the problems outside it? If it were, I could live in blissful delusion, believing that peace is defined as the absence of conflict. Nothing of that sort, however, leads to any genuine truth. Authentic peace involves the constant struggle for the good. How I struggled chasing after my own good rather than the Creator's goodness.

"Save me because of your mercy."

By now a pattern had surfaced. In 2019, I was again inside a church, one near Palermo, Sicily, just one mile from the Tyrrhenian Sea. A religious sister was guiding me on a directed retreat and gave me points to pray with for the day. "How long?" She asked me this question in relation to how much longer I thought I could limp through my own vocation as a Jesuit priest and young scholar. How much longer could I sustain living with one foot in the door and the other outside of the demands of religious life? Did

I have the freedom to hear whatever Jesus had to say to me? As it turned out, I had little freedom at that time. It was like living in a perpetual state of Lent and never Easter. But this was okay.

Lent can be a sacred time to recognize unfreedoms. Lent can be a time to gently place down those knapsacks, as the Salish people do when they enter their sacred sweats.

Praying with these questions, I found myself kneeling by a pew before the crucifix. I closed my eyes and entered into what Ignatius of Loyola calls a contemplation. This style of Ignatian prayer is a meditation based on one's imagination, always in search of a meaningful conversation with Jesus. Deep in prayer, I imagined myself dressed in a clerical shirt with a ragged trench coat covering me against the cold as I lay near a gutter on the cold asphalt. With one hand I held tightly to a bottle of whiskey, while the other held onto a vulgar magazine. I felt emotionally tired, physically weary, and without a spiritual home.

After a few moments, the prayer got very real as I turned to gaze at Jesus nailed on the cross. What a scene! Me on the ground by the gutter, and Jesus nailed on the cross. Jesus looked at me from the vantage point of the cross, and said quietly and clearly, "Get up. You need to get up." To which I responded, without much hesitation, "No." He told me a second time, "Get up." Again I replied, "No, thanks. I'm tired." This stalemate went back and forth for a few minutes, with neither of us gaining an advantage over the other until a breakthrough arrived. Jesus did not win me over by logic, but by persistence. He said in my prayer, "I know that you are tired, and that you can't get up. I'm telling you that you need to get up anyway."

I can only explain these moments as grace. I immediately understood what Christ, there on the cross, was asking of me. In my complete weakness, having reached a limit in my spiritual life, Jesus was offering me his redemptive grace for the hundredth time in my life. He was inviting me into companionship within my brokenness and not in spite of it. What else could I do but walk with him a little longer and perhaps a little further down this unknown path?

Precisely within lament, the psalmist recognizes God's saving hand. "Turn back, LORD, rescue my soul; save me because of your mercy."

Lent has the potential to become a time of contemplative prayer. We are invited to build an imaginary enclosure where God sets the boundary. God becomes the protective fence that surrounds us while we build a door where love is allowed in and love is allowed out. The key is to know where we are and with whom—but we do not always have to know why.

4

Fear of the Lord

> I will instruct you and show you the way you
> should walk,
> give you counsel with my eye upon you.
> Do not be like a horse or a mule, without
> understanding;
> with bit and bridle their temper is
> curbed,
> else they will not come to you.
>
> Psalm 32:8–9

Consider the ancient Appian Way that stretches from Rome to the Adriatic coast at Brindisi. The 350-mile journey might seem too far to complete, even for a willing sojourner. But what joy and relief to reach the destination after crossing such vast distance.

The path to wholeness, which Scripture understands as maturing in one's humanity, can appear like a long, narrow road. The second Penitential Psalm merits returning to for prayer and council throughout the length of Lent. Our previous psalm, Psalm 6, teased out the prolonged nature of lament: "LORD, how long?" Along that path is a hard truth that requires a lifetime to lean into, one that this second Penitential Psalm presents clearly. "I will instruct you and show you the way you should walk." If, however, you identify with the stubborn horse, or with the intelligent and more stubborn mule, acquiring the character to be taught and guided by the Spirit will require even greater patience.

Scripture, especially in the wisdom literature, provides a kind of first instruction, a grounding principle for a person growing in their faith, as a path toward wholeness. For example, "The beginning of wisdom is fear of the LORD" (Prov 9:10). The second half of this famous verse is less known, "And knowledge of the Holy One is understanding." It has nothing to do with our common use of the word *fear*. The phrase, "fear of the LORD," in every instance implies a posture of reverence before the mystery confronted. Humble respect is another way to say the same thing.

A dramatic example of this lesson may be gleaned from the Book of Job. Job is confronted by the loss of everything dear to him except three things: his wife, his ability to question God, and his reverence for the mystery he encounters. We might ask whether Job is on the verge of losing his faith too. Probably not, but he does question the core of that faith passionately.

The wager at the beginning of this parable on wisdom revolves around the consequences of suffering. A bet is made between God and "the Satan." In the Book of Job, Satan functions as a heavenly prosecutor who serves an accusatorial role against humans. At this point in the Bible, this shadowy figure is not quite defined as the origin of evil that will develop later in the Christian tradition.

Early in the text, Job loses the support of his wife in his quest for the justification of God's actions. These actions appear unjust or questionable to Job, who has lost everything. Her actual comment is terse, "Are you still holding to your innocence? Curse God and die!" (Job 2:9). Job's wife offers another point of view, though, as she brings to her partner a voice of mercy and a different kind of wisdom. Many recent studies see the wife as a catalyst for Job to move beyond justification to one of acceptance before a mystery not fully understood. While Job accepts his fate, he still wants answers to that fate and thus places conditions set by him alone. His wife reminds him that he will not find a satisfactory answer for all his suffering. And she is not wrong. The need for answers often takes possession of one's quest in life, but reverence before a mystery might bring a far greater spiritual balm, like the one Job sought. "I will . . . give you counsel," says the divine voice, "with my eye upon you."

A second glance at the book's opening tension reveals that the wager between God and Satan does not focus on the nature of suffering but on Job's character. Will Job shake? Will he break down and curse God, like he curses the day of his own birth (Job 3:3–4)? No. He does not break down to a point of no return. Instead,

Job's lament, presented through the questioning of the Almighty One, continues for forty-two chapters.

The ending of Job is one of literature's masterpieces—one often misrepresented as remorse, which is far from the richer meaning. Job finally learns a costly lesson. The words from the second Penitential Psalm, "I will instruct you," have never been truer than they were for Job by the end of his grievance against God. After God gives the final response to his servant Job—one that could easily be interpreted as a nonresponse—Job replies with what seems to be his final acceptance. Has Job lifted his white flag of surrender?

Job has assumed that he was placing God on trial for most of the book, and that his prosecution would at the very least squeeze out a confession from the defendant. But it turns out that Job has been the one on trial the whole time. These are Job's last words: "By hearsay I had heard of you, but now my eye has seen you. Therefore I disown what I have said, and repent in dust and ashes" (Job 42:5–6). It seems as if the case is closed.

In fact, Job is now ready to begin again.

The last verse of Job's speech in the Hebrew is gibberish. It sounds something like this: "Therefore / I reject / I mourn / dust and ash." Our natural tendency is to force a meaningful syntax on the text, as we often force meaning onto situations that overwhelm us. My own interpretation considers the wisdom of Job. It is slight conjecture, but true to Job's struggle in wrestling with himself for forty-two chapters. It makes more sense to interpret Job's last thoughts with something true to his saga. For example: "My final verdict is this:

I reject everything I have said until now about God. I will go back and reconsider this mortal life with God at the center instead of me."

Two things happen with this alternative ending. First, it shows how God has been instructing Job the whole time, as the psalm suggests, "I will show you the way you should walk." Second, it reveals the richer meaning of the fear of the Lord as reverence before a mystery confronted.

Job learns little about the nature of suffering and its ultimate purpose. What he does grasp, however, is how to think about the problem again, returning to the beginning of his questioning in order to rethink everything. What has changed? Neither God nor any of Job's losses. The only thing that changes is Job. "Do not be like a horse or a mule, without understanding; with bit and bridle their temper is curbed, else they will not come to you."

5

The Lord's Arrows

LORD, do not punish me in your anger;
  in your wrath do not chastise me!
Your arrows have sunk deep in me;
  your hand has come down upon me.
There is no wholesomeness in my flesh
    because of your anger;
  there is no health in my bones because
    of my sin.
My iniquities overwhelm me,
  a burden too heavy for me.

Psalm 38:2–5

I

This third Penitential Psalm stands out for its strong and effective medicine. Psalm 38 is made up of twenty-three verses, of which twenty-two seem hopeless. Fortunately, the overall tone is redeemed by the last verse, which reminds the hearer there might be a way out of a hopeless situation.

The longer you stay with a psalm like this, the more you begin to understand the whole point of the meditation. Some circumstance in life can bring us to realize that we have reached a state of helplessness that has no remedy. Those of us who have experienced rock bottom will recognize this emotion. For us, the psalm's harsh words ring true. At the same time, however, the structure of the hymn can serve as healing balm to a person (or a people) in desperation. Whoever wrote this psalm left us a reminder that whatever we suffer, the psalmist also experienced.

This is a good point to remember that in the biblical tradition, lament is always a prayer. It carries an implicit impulse for hope, even when the person lamenting perceives hope's absence.

On further reflection, we find a curious use of language from the psalm: "Your arrows have sunk deep in me; your hand has come down upon me." These are not your typical arrows. They represent the warrior and warfare familiar to the ancient writer. God as a warrior was a common motif. God's wrath can fall on anyone, especially one in need of repentance. It is not the dominant image we carry today about God, but it is a biblical one, and it merits some thought and reflection. The arrows that struck down the psalmist in this lament belong to no one else but God.

These arrows shoot straight from the divine hand. The implication is that God does not and will not spare us from great anguish in life. But this truth pierces even deeper. The psalm speaks of bodily harm, an illness so severe that the person found herself on her deathbed: "Foul and festering are my sores because of my folly" (Ps 38:6). Is there another way to think of these arrows? Perhaps not as inflicting a flesh wound, but an injury to one's spirit? Both kinds of woundedness merit attention.

The image of being struck down by a divine arrow may also imply that we are meant to bring a message to the world about God's mercy—that we are part of a small circle of emissaries of God's light. If this is the case, we are blessed, because the Lord's arrow is guaranteed to pierce us first. There are numerous examples of this in Scripture, beginning with Job and the psalms. These form part of the wisdom corpus of biblical literature. But we can also skip forward to Mary, whom the Gospels present as a wisdom figure in her own right. The hand of God upon someone, biblically speaking, was not the touch of physical death but the experience of a great spiritual death that needed to take place within you. Is the purpose of the Lord's arrow to make us suffer? No, but we will suffer. Is its purpose to teach us some moral lesson? No, but we will learn a great lesson, for ourselves and for others.

What then is the arrow's purpose? It may function as a sign that we are doing God's work. It is a crude reminder for our soul to keep at it with humility, because the recompense we seek is with God in some other place, and not necessarily in the material now.

"Your arrows have sunk deep in me."

Mary's own soul was pierced. The Gospel reads that a sword rather than an arrow pierced Our Lady. Two elders who mostly resided within the temple in Jerusalem brought messages to the Holy Family about Jesus. The last words that the prophet Simeon says to Mary are haunting: "Behold, this child is destined for the fall and rise of many in Israel, and to be a sign that will be contradicted." Then comes a message directly aimed at Mary: "(and you yourself a sword will pierce) so that the thoughts of many hearts may be revealed" (Luke 2:34–35). As any good commentary will say, wisdom figures are meant to feel what God feels, and Mary is no exception.

Everything that Mary will face in her life stays within a reflective space known to her alone. There are awe-inspiring events that are associated with Advent, such as the divine announcement made to the shepherds in the field about the anointed child born to the world. They hear a host of angels singing, "Glory to God in the highest." When the shepherds run to inform Mary about all of this, Luke provides a single note of commentary: "Mary kept all these things, reflecting on them in her heart" (Luke 2:19). As we turn to our Lenten theme, however, in the same chapter Mary has heard a strange and alarming warning from Simeon. Luke also reveals that the twelve-year-old Jesus caused his parents grief and anxiety by staying behind in Jerusalem without telling them. How is the Holy Mother of the Holy Child going to deal with the strange path she now faces? Luke writes again the same note of commentary, "And his mother kept all these things in her heart" (Luke 2:51).

The interior life is a world unto itself. Mary is pierced by God and yet within her heart she made a space that allowed her to carry a constant meditation, an unbroken vigil for the mysterious presence of God at work. Even—and especially—when lament and sadness are involved.

II

I am stooped and deeply bowed;
every day I go about mourning.
My loins burn with fever;
there is no wholesomeness in my flesh.
I am numb and utterly crushed;
I wail with anguish of heart.
My Lord, my deepest yearning is before you;
my groaning is not hidden from you.

Psalm 38:7–10

The first two years of Jesuit training are called the novitiate. When a young Jesuit in formation enters, his class varies in size and personality. My class began with seven men and by the end of two years we were down to five. Those who remained toward the end of the novitiate were all musicians. Each of us was very different from the others, but together we were called "the musical class." Each one brought to the table a unique perspective—a tune of our own. At the end of our novitiate experience, the novice master guided the five of us in one final group meditation through a creative, Spirit-led form of communal prayer.

"My Lord, my deepest yearning is before you; my groaning is not hidden from you."

It was called the Angel's Seal. The goal of this prayer exercise was to collectively affirm each other in our vocation as we leapt into the next step in Jesuit formation. Each took a turn as one person's name was said aloud; meanwhile, the rest of the group prayed silently for that person. We were asked to allow an image or symbol to surface in our imagination as we prayed. This symbol could be something representative of our prayer for that individual. Two of these reflections stand out to me now, as I pray with the words of the third Penitential Psalm.

The first image comes from a classmate who described a scene in which I stood still and gently held a vase. As my novice bother described it, I held a beautiful porcelain vase in my hands, beaming in childlike delight. Suddenly, I dropped it. The vase shattered into pieces on the floor before me. My smile was gone. In the next scene, Jesus was there with me as he gently placed the restored vase back into my hands, the one I had just shattered into pieces. As I held this restored vase, you could see the cracks, the lines where the vase came together like a puzzle—but the vase was perfectly intact, and my smile returned too. I was happy-sad. The vase represented my vocation, something fragile but always capable of staying in once piece through Jesus's intervention.

I was not prepared for the second image about me that surfaced through our communal prayer. A classmate who knew me better than the others painted a dramatic scene. I was in the midst of hundreds of other Native American warriors on horseback, racing forward into battle. The enemy's position could not be seen, but an arrow came from their side and struck me through my chest, into my heart. My classmate slowed down and said clearly, "I wish you could have seen what I saw. It was an epic battle." He then said, "The arrow was poverty, and you were defeated."

How does one defeat poverty? "I am numb and utterly crushed; I wail with anguish of heart."

Fr. Joe Tetlow, SJ, a master of directing St. Ignatius of Loyola's *Spiritual Exercises*, once pointed to the crucifix while giving a talk to retreatants engaged in eight days of prayer. He said, "Look, folks, in case you were wondering how it ended for Jesus, it was a failure. His life ended defeated on the cross." We are not always meant to win. In fact, being struck by the divine arrow is God's way of bringing you right into the heart of the Son's redemptive mystery.

There is no actual resolution in this psalm. All that stands out is the last line, a slight glimmer of hope:

"Come quickly to help me, my Lord and my salvation!" (Ps 38:23). That's it. But it is a powerful ending, a prayer meant to acknowledge that help is needed, and the psalmist is ready to seek it out. The last words of the psalm are barely enough to raise our hope compared to the weight of all the other verses. But this, too, becomes a mystery. In sacred math, can a small dot of faith with the prospect of hope outweigh the lived experience of suffering? That seems to be the truth of the cross. Hope does outweigh the anguish lived. This might be upsetting to us, but it is true for those who have experienced the dynamic of pain and faith, of lament and hope. It remains true for the person who laments while retaining their faith.

In some ways, it is perfectly understandable to consider the last verse of the psalm a small prayer: "Help me, O Lord." What we know, however, is that this calling out to God as "Lord" in the Greek text of this psalm reveals the vocative case ending. This means it may be translated "O Lord!" but also as "my Lord!" This sounds like splitting hairs, but the New American Bible translation does translate the final verse in this way: "Come quickly to help me, *my Lord and my salvation*!" (Ps 38:23). It is the "my Lord and my salvation!" that is strikingly similar to the last words from the Apostle Thomas when Jesus appeared to his disciples after his resurrection. The Gospel of John records the memory of a shocked Thomas, who cries out as he transitions from disbelief to belief, "My Lord and my God!" (John 20:28). This simple line, this one single verse, becomes the definitive christological statement for the entire Gospel of John about the nature of Jesus's divinity and union with the Father.

In times of trouble, the best prayer we can say is to call out like children to the one who waits patiently to be called upon. Small prayers can also be the most powerful ones.

6

Honesty

For the leader. A psalm of David, when
Nathan the prophet came to him, after he
had gone in to Bathsheba.

Psalm 51:1–2

I

This fourth Penitential Palm is the most famous of the seven. Psalm 51 is set apart as a key psalm within the Divine Office, the church's official prayer for priests, the religious, and the faithful. Every Friday throughout the year the Divine Office opens morning prayer with this psalm. Its message resonates in the form of lament—but not like the other six Penitential Palms. Guilt begins this lament, followed by remorse and ownership of personal sin and its social impact. Guilt is so prominent in the first half of the psalm that

I have often felt repulsed by its emphasis on a personal *mea culpa*. No wonder that during Lent, Psalm 51 provides the guiding theme for the season designated as a cycle of guilt-remorse-forgiveness. But there is wisdom within and beyond this cycle found in the psalm as well, and we are invited to unravel its instructive opening lines.

The informative lines at the beginning of some psalms are usually ignored. They provide notes for how the psalm was sung in antiquity, or for their particular style. We do not know exactly how the original tune or score was performed in the temple or ancient synagogue. What we do know is the literary sense of the psalm that the original author suggested for a particular piece. Psalm 51, for example, opens with a cue in the critical notes themselves: "[A reminder] for the [choir] leader: a David hymn, when Nathan came to him, after [David] had gone to Bathsheba." While several psalms provide introductions for the choir leader, few provide such specific notes that set the tone like this one. The original author reminds us to enter into this lament by recalling David's critical offense in his life of service to God and Israel. David is God's servant, and much is expected of him.

Recall the passage in which the prophet Nathan reminds David of the gravity of his actions (2 Sam 12). In the previous chapter, David had crossed a line. He showed no remorse, but instead tried to cover his adultery by murdering Bathsheba's husband, Uriah. David was still campaigning for his kingdom, but he was already king with more power than he could fathom.

"I gave you your lord's house and your lord's wives for your own," God said to David, "and if this were not enough, I could count up for you still more" (2 Sam 12:8). God revealed to David that the gravity of his offence was clear, but somehow David remained blind to it. The outrage was twofold. First, the fact that David slept with Bathsheba, a beautiful woman for whom he had lusted and with whom he committed adultery; and second, Nathan's accusation of David was about the circumstances *around* this grave offence.

"Secretly," says the psalmist, "you teach me wisdom" (Ps 51:8).

David was rich, while Uriah was poor. David had everything, including real power to wield. Uriah had only two things—his integrity and his wife. When David realized that Bathsheba was pregnant by him, he tried all the usual tricks to hide his deed. When he could not deceive Uriah, due to the Uriah's character, David engineered Uriah's death—the death of his own faithful servant—in order to conceal his guilt. These actions angered the higher power. Nathan the prophet worked his way into David's predicament through a parable describing a situation concerning two men, one rich and the other poor.

> The rich man had flocks and herds in great numbers. But the poor man had nothing at all except one little ewe lamb that he had bought. He nourished her, and she grew up with him and his children. Of what little he had she ate; from his own cup she drank; in

> his bosom she slept; she was like a daughter to him. Now, a visitor came to the rich man, but he spared his own flocks and herds to prepare a meal for the traveler who had come to him: he took the poor man's ewe lamb and prepared it for the one who had come to him. (2 Sam 12:2–4)

David became outraged at this parable. He unconsciously perceived the moral situation as God would. In the parable, the rich man took what he wanted from the poor one, without consequences and without empathy. David reacted by saying that the only correct punishment for the rich man in the parable was death. The scene ends with a final resolution from Nathan: "You are the man!" (2 Sam 12:7).

What stands out? Against his own will, David was guided by God to a path of honesty. He was led to embrace his own deeds, whether they were filled with integrity or hopelessly misguided. This bending of the will toward raw honesty is the opening tone for the fourth Penitential Psalm. It opens with a reminder of submission to the moral arc of the universe that bends toward justice. The moral arc, however, also bends toward mercy. Perhaps submission is the wrong word—as if someone were constantly beaten down by another's will. It's more like surrender; we are meant to surrender to the moral arc of the universe that bends toward mercy.

II

Have mercy on me, God, in accord with
your merciful love;
in your abundant compassion blot out
my transgressions.
Thoroughly wash away my guilt;
and from my sin cleanse me.
For I know my transgressions;
my sin is always before me.

Psalm 51:3–5

The opening lines of the psalm appeal directly to God. The Hebrew offers a nuanced approach from three different nouns to capture the nature of God. Our English translations are limited to words like *pity*, *compassion*, and *mercy*. Imagine a different opening: "Have *mercy* on me, God, with your merciful *mercy*, and with your abundant *mercy* remove my offence." Another attempt to translate the opening line could be, "Have *compassion* on me, God, with your committed *compassion*, and in your rich *compassion* blot out my transgression." What stands out is the amplified use of words that relate to mercy or compassion as a uniquely divine quality.

The psalm makes a point to show how mercy and God are interchangeable. One defines the other in this Penitential Psalm. Here we have unlocked a guiding principle for Psalm 51, as well as for Lent. The penitent discovers the freedom and courage necessary to be honest about everything. There is no fear of hiding or of exposing all of one's iniquity, because the penitent has finally felt in his or her bones that God is synonymous with merciful compassion. There will be consequences to deal with later, but these will be just before a mysterious God revealed as mercy.

This realization changes everything. I have directed dozens of individuals through the *Spiritual Exercises*. The majority have struggled to pray with a healthy and robust imagination of God. This presents a wall, or spiritual block, at the beginning of the long spiritual retreat they have expressed interest in completing. The foundational starting points that begin the retreat require honesty about ourselves, and about our own history of prayer and the image of God we have carried over the years. Ignatius believed that if the retreatant did not begin with an image of God grounded in unwavering mercy, their prayer would suffer from an overly burdened emphasis on personal sin. But if their image of God was more in line with the biblical accounts, even guilt could eventually guide them to an experience of honesty that in turn becomes hope.

With this understanding of the Creator, the psalmist is able to take full ownership of his actions without fear. "For I know my transgressions."

III

Behold, you desire true sincerity;
and secretly you teach me wisdom.

Cleanse me with hyssop, that I may be pure;
wash me, and I will be whiter than
snow.
You will let me hear gladness and joy;
the bones you have crushed will
rejoice.

Psalm 51:8–10

In the long and conflicted history between the Catholic Church and Native Americans, honesty has not been at the center of the relationship. While this might sound like a generalization, and without naming any specific tribe, the early missionary activity held tight to the belief that if they chipped away slowly at Indian culture, the native peoples would benefit in the long run. Some early missionaries, it is true, learned the local language and helped to preserve the indigenous culture through printed dictionaries. These records helped document some of the First Peoples' mother tongues. Nonetheless, the dominant feeling was that native people needed to integrate and quickly become both Western and Christian. What held this conviction together was a perennial sense of moral certitude held by those of European decent, followed by contempt for the old ways of the Native Americans. The unquestioned way of Western civilization was superior to the native ways, according to those who held with moral certitude that no other path existed.

If we think back on the conflict David felt within himself because of Uriah, something rises to the surface. Nathan's parable exposed the madness of having the poor man's only ewe slaughtered. The poor man had one comfort to his name. Uriah had one comfort, Bathsheba, and she was taken from him. Likewise, the early North American tribes possessed one thing that provided immense psychological and spiritual consolation: their native culture as a way to express themselves in a dignified manner. The one thing they had was slowly taken from them over time. The church, it is now recognized increasingly through hindsight, was often the primary tool the United States government relied on to make that possible.

"For I know my transgressions; my sin is always before me."

A group of benefactors recently asked me why the suicide rates on reservations are often higher than the national average. I needed time to think of a response. The questions they were asking are the tip of the iceberg; once you begin to talk on this sensitive subject, it's like peeling away at an onion one layer after another. My response, therefore, was nuanced. I tried my best to share a few brief stories.

At present I am the pastor of St. Ignatius Mission Parish, a Catholic Jesuit mission in continuous existence since 1854 on the Flathead Indian Reservation of western Montana. Just recently the leader of our prayer chain at the parish posted the following petition:

> For Jenny's sixteen-year-old great-granddaughter, Maggie, who is struggling emotionally and mentally. For Nancy, who is raising her and at a loss on how to help her.

> For all youth who struggle on this day to find hope and a purpose in life. Does anyone have an idea on how to gather this age group for discussion, witness, and fellowship? They're not coming to church. Does Tribal Health have resources? Does the school? I'm just grasping at straws. Lord Jesus Christ, we ask you to shed light on this situation.

And then there was another prayer request the following week: "Please pray for Sandra who's in Alaska, helping her patients and their community deal with a rash of suicides."

Two weeks ago, as I write this, we offered the Mass for a twelve-year-old girl who committed suicide on a nearby reservation.

Our parish does not have a direct ministry to serve those who suffer from mental illness. We do some preventative work through grief support and events for the youth, but this is so minimal. What becomes clear, however, is how many of our parishioners are affected by cases or by victims they hear about from neighbors and family.

I have visited and spent time with several women in recovery. Most of them were moms. On one of these occasions, I ended up making a pastoral visit for someone committed to a psych ward in Missoula. She happened to live on the reservation near the church. Afterward, this mother came around for several weeks after our initial visit to the hospital just to check in and hang out. Her whole immediate family came with her on these visits. She was looking for a kind face, perhaps the gentle reminder of human contact from a Good Samaritan.

The research from tribal communities and people with experience in this line of work presents two key factors as to why the suicide rate is higher than the national average for Native Americans on reservations. These are the loss of connection through culture, and the prevalence of generational trauma. I believe this to be true, and if it is true, a healthier community around issues of mental health will involve the prevalence of generational healing. Everyone wants to see a well-funded program with enough key structures to provide a quick fix. Benefactors and do-gooders often hope to relieve themselves of the guilt that comes from turning a blind eye to our neighbors in pain. But the solution takes a different form completely. It will take effort from many people, organizations, and communities over several generations to heal and respond to generations of trauma.

A generation after us might one day sing with the psalmist, "You will let me hear gladness and joy; the bones you have crushed will rejoice." There is a sense of liberation in letting go and understanding that "gladness and joy" might not happen in this lifetime, but it may in the next.

Our present psalm makes a reference to an old ritualistic tool used for sacrificial purification, which offers a reset for the individual and society. "Cleanse me with hyssop, that I may be pure; wash me, and I will be whiter than snow."

Hyssop was used in ancient rituals because the shape of the hyssop branch made a perfect sprinkling tool to dip into the blood of the sacrifice and splash onto the recipient. Blood in the ancient world worked like detergent. Through it, with belief and prayer, sin and harm could be cleansed through the sacrifice that had been made. The greater the harm, the greater the sacrifice needed. In the Fourth Gospel, John makes this connection to Jesus on the cross as the sacrificial lamb slain for the world.

> After this, aware that everything was now finished, in order that the scripture might be fulfilled, Jesus said, "I thirst." There was a vessel filled with common wine. So they put a sponge soaked in wine on a sprig of hyssop and put it up to his mouth. When Jesus had taken the wine, he said, "It is finished." And bowing his head, he handed over the spirit. (John 19:28–30)

Generational healing is meant for the world, past and future. Jesus's sacrifice on the cross was meant to fully redirect the sinner and the society. The greater the harm, the greater the sacrifice—so goes the ancient theological framework. But it's true: Psalm 51 recognizes the imbalance in our communities when sin goes unaddressed. Since the greatest sacrifice has been offered already, and since the Eucharist is a continuation of that one sacrifice already made, we are truly a free people. What a mystery to reclaim this overlooked truth! This mystery remains buried beneath layers of false guarantees from society that promise liberation outside of the sacrifice of the cross.

IV

Restore to me the gladness of your
 salvation;
 uphold me with a willing spirit....
For you do not desire sacrifice or I would
 give it;
 a burnt offering you would not accept.
My sacrifice, O God, is a contrite spirit;
 a contrite, humbled heart, O God, you
 will not scorn.

Psalm 51:14, 18–19

The psalm ends with a bold acknowledgment of having reached a place of contrition, and what's more, a humbled heart. Humility's counterpart is pride. The psalmist has taken a long journey to where this lament ends, with a powerful pull toward hope. Keep me lifted up, says the psalmist: "Uphold me with a willing spirit." A willing spirit captures the desired hope during Lent. What each penitent ultimately desires is a spirit capable of pushing forward through every high and low that life presents. A willing spirit sounds like energy from a quiet source that sustains. It is the opposite of giving up.

As a trajectory, the psalm has taken this reader through many valleys. What has emerged? The lament began with sensations of guilt and ownership of transgressions. But this only skims the surface of what this lament has unearthed. Words filled with depth come to mind, like *honesty* and *mercy*. For difficult cases and conflicted histories, there is no other place to begin reconciliation except through honesty and mercy.

Other themes emerge too, such as the need for contact, for human-to-human connection as a place where God reveals his divine presence. But for places where brokenness has held its ground in one form or another, this psalm brings out the lament for generational healing.

Great blessing flows from spending time with the most famous of the Penitential Psalms. Its themes release a transformative meditation for a Lenten pilgrimage. Through these lamentations, Lent provides us a return path that offers generational healing and a roadmap to reconnection.

7

Santiago

The prayer of one afflicted and wasting away whose anguish is poured out before the Lord.

For my days vanish like smoke;
   my bones burn away as in a furnace.
I am like a desert owl, like an owl among
      the ruins.
   I eat ashes like bread, mingle my drink
      with tears.
Because of your furious wrath,
   you lifted me up just to cast me down.
My days are like a lengthening shadow;
   I wither like the grass.

Psalm 102:4, 7, 10–12

I

The fifth Penitential Psalm does not begin with a hopeful tone. It is as if we have come full circle, returning to a lament of helplessness. Our previous Penitential Psalm, Psalm 51, ended with a radical belief in the "willing spirit" that gathers enough strength to push forward. But the first part of Psalm 102 is a prayer on the verge of giving up.

Personal sin or the brokenness of a community are not the cause of this lament. The psalmist depicts someone wasting away both physically and psychologically. There is a strong sense of slipping away, not on account of age, but apparently on account of poor health and isolation. Here is a lament dependent on the realization of our short lifespan and its lack of significance—like vanishing smoke rather than something eternal.

Think of liminal space. What happens in the next life? This question has been asked since humanity first organized itself to reflect on these questions of the spirit. In the ancient world, there were hints that the human soul could live on after death and perhaps attach itself to the eternal spirit world. There was no guarantee, however. The general belief of the faithful, as depicted in the psalms, held onto a lingering doubt that life could exist beyond the natural limits of mortality. Powerful deities were eternal, but mere mortals fell into a category described as those who "wither like the grass."

Traditionally speaking, the person in this psalm was thought to be the one who has nothing else but God to rely on for survival. Who could blame the psalmist for struggling through his reflections, whether life continued on or ended with his present illness? What grave poverty must the psalmist have been experiencing to believe that trust in the Lord was limited to this life alone. Could faith and hope could grow from that conclusion? God is eternal, but am I?

On the reservation where I live, death is as common as the strange sky of this land. Just these past few weeks, as I write this, we have experienced a wave of deaths in the community. One person lived into his nineties, while another one lived for just a few short months. I spoke at a service held for the death of the baby. I was asked to say a few words of consolation in front of the parents and extended family who had just lost their four-month-old. What words could provide solace to the family's grief? The more tragic the loss, the more pressing the question: What is the value of life when death can effortlessly swallow it up? Where is hope? As the psalmist cried out, "You lifted me up just to cast me down"—like this baby brought into life only to pass away four months later.

"I eat ashes like bread, mingle my drink with tears."

Santiago has been on my mind. The name is beautifully composed of *San*, meaning "saint" in Spanish, and *Yago*, meaning "James." It was the name of my cousin's first baby boy. I met him at my first Mass as a newly ordained Jesuit priest. His parents asked me if I could baptize their newborn as they presented him formally for the first time in public. That first Mass was held at San Gabriel Mission, in the old mission church first set up by the Franciscans and built through the labor of local Gabrielino-Tongva tribe.

It seemed to me that Santiago was the most well-behaved baby that ever existed. He never cried or made a fuss about anything, and he barely opened his eyes. I asked my cousin that day why Santiago was so easy, and he told me that he was always like that at home too. He just slept a lot.

I thought nothing of this until later. Santiago was not just well-behaved and relaxed at his baptism. His infant body was conserving whatever energy it had because he was born with a rare type of cancer that had gone undetected. For the next four years, Santiago would be in and out of hospitals, his parents right there with him, fighting for every ounce of hope they could gather. One of his aunties would tell me often that even if there was a 1 percent chance of survival, everything should be done to save his life—everything and anything. At what point is the mortal life marked by illness meant to be just that: temporal and limited?

It was Santiago himself who would eventually understand his own fate. At the age of four he would coach his own family to slowly let go. His older sister was the first one to see the big picture. She wanted her little brother to be okay, to be with God and to suffer no longer. Dad was next. His "willing spirit" reached a point of surrender—not giving up, but surrendering to whatever happened next. Last to be convinced were his aunties and mother. Toward the end, Santiago had a talk with his mother. She had reached her limit, and did not know whether to continue fighting, to move across the country for more doctors, hospitals, and treatment proposals, or to let go. The voice of discernment came through Santiago himself. He told his mom a profound truth, "I'm going to be okay, and it's okay to let go."

II

Of old you laid the earth's foundations;
the heavens are the work of your
hands.
They perish, but you remain;
they all wear out like a garment;
Like clothing you change them and they
are changed,
but you are the same, your years have
no end.
May the children of your servants live on;
may their descendants live in your
presence.

Psalm 102:26–29

A few months after Santiago's passing, I was asked to participate in a pilgrimage, accompanying a group of young seminarians from Naples, Italy. We formed a pilgrim cohort traveling all the way from the Naples airport to Spain. We walked a portion of the famous El Camino a Santiago de Compostela, the Way of St. James. The tomb of Santiago was our final destination.

The journey itself was typical of any good pilgrimage. Four characteristics come to mind: slowness, movement, purpose, and prayer. In fact, Lent is a perfect time to make a spiritual pilgrimage marked with these same characteristics to embark on a journey of the soul.

The first thing I noticed was the Spanish landscape. Carving out the time to notice the green horizon of mountains was the one thing that helped slow down my mind and heart a little. Creation has a way of introducing humility, and the mountains and valleys share a secret from the earliest moments of the earth's formation. As Psalm 102:26 says, "Of old you laid the earth's foundations; the heavens are the work of your hands." This thought, however, brings little comfort to the psalmist. For what can be more everlasting than mountains and a heavenly skyline? But all created things are not meant to last, as the psalm goes on to say: "They perish, but you remain" (Ps 102:27).

Only God is eternal—period. Whatever is connected to God may somehow continue to live on, and whatever is not must perish as all things perish.

I noticed a movement within myself during the pilgrimage. Something changed. I could sense a deep yearning to understand the purpose of this small pilgrimage. I began to pray with Santiago in mind—my baby cousin who had passed away. After all, the entire pilgrimage was held to honor his patron saint. Santiago became my spiritual companion along the journey to the Cathedral of Santiago. I prayed for everyone: his family, his parents, and especially for myself. How does one grieve the loss of a child? When is the lament complete? Does the experience test one's faith or cause one to lose it?

Please, Santiago, pray for us on this pilgrimage of life.

I even selfishly prayed for myself, a lot. Feeling lost with the next phase of my life's journey, I continued to move forward. About a quarter of the pilgrimage still remained before we would reach the tomb of St. James. At that moment, Santiago's voice broke though as clear as the divine voice from the transfiguration scene in the Gospels. What fell into my heart were my little cousin's words speaking to me: "I'm okay, and everything is going to be okay." A full awareness of the experience of faith penetrated to my core. Santiago was in a better place now than all of us here walking on the foundations of the earth.

It is good to think of the communion of saints as often as possible. A lament without faith may lead to despair and, conversely, a lament with faith may lead to a place of hope. A pilgrimage, by definition, cannot be made alone. You must walk with someone. This becomes a radical concept of faith because it provides a way to break the despair of fading away like the withering grass. The psalmist reached this insight through a plea for his descendants. "May the children of your servants live on; may their descendants live in your presence" (Ps 102:29). If our collective hope is not wrapped up somehow within the hope of a community, not just our own faith journey, then our faith remains in vain. In Christian terms, the sentiment "may the children of your servants live on" is laid on the groundwork of Christ. Discipleship becomes a way to keep the faith, to pass it on to the next generation and to continue to stay in communion with all the saints, especially those who have passed away.

Santiago, pray for us.

8

Hope

A song of ascents.

Out of the depths I call to you, LORD;
   Lord, hear my cry!
May your ears be attentive
   to my cry for mercy.
If you, LORD, keep account of sins,
   Lord, who can stand?

But with you is forgiveness
   and so you are revered.

I wait for the LORD,
   my soul waits
   and I hope for his word.
My soul looks for the Lord
   more than sentinels for daybreak.
More than sentinels for daybreak,
   let Israel hope in the LORD,

For with the LORD is mercy,
    with him is plenteous redemption,
And he will redeem Israel
    from all its sins.

Psalm 130:1–8

The penultimate Penitential Psalm demands time and consideration in its entirety. It should be recited in prayer over and over again, because it presents a defining model for a people of faith. The introductory verse calls it "a psalm of ascents." Psalms 120—135 are all considered psalms of ascent. Their original use was probably for pilgrims on their way to visit the holy temple in Jerusalem. They were recited on pilgrimage to Zion.

This hymn, however, may be viewed as either a psalm of thanksgiving in acknowledgment of being rescued, or as a Penitential Psalm due to the recognition of a merciful God. The opening verse is striking: "Out of the depths I call to you." These depths make us think of another place in the Bible—they were very familiar to the reluctant servant of the Lord, the Old Testament prophet Jonah.

There are two versions of Jonah's character. One version is the tired-out prophet, nervous to be working for what he saw as a pushover God. According to the prophet, God was inconsistent in judgement and reckless in granting pardon. "But with you is forgiveness and so you are revered," says the psalmist. Jonah, in striking contrast, does not see this God, except when he is in need of deliverance himself.

The second version of Jonah is the poet who cries

out after being swallowed by the great fish monster. From the depths of the waters, he sings:

> I went down to the roots of the mountains;
> to the land whose bars closed behind me
> forever,
> But you brought my life up from the pit,
> O LORD, my God.
>
> When I became faint,
> I remembered the LORD;
> My prayer came to you
> in your holy temple. (Jonah 2:7–8)

The range of God's presence stands out. Here was Jonah in the pits, at the gates of the netherworld, where he began to remember that the Lord might hear him. Jonah imagined that his prayer traveled all the way to the holy temple, the central conduit of God's grace, something like God's headquarters on earth to hear and receive prayers. Perhaps God rejected some prayers sent there, as if it were like a post office of the spirit world. The best Jonah could do was to imagine how the Lord may or may not respond to his predicament. According to Jonah's prayer of thanksgiving, God's presence never left his servant, wherever he was found. God waited for Jonah to notice him—even in the depths of the pit.

To understand Psalm 130 is to understand Jonah's tension in life. Jonah's tension in his service to God and his mission to the sinful citizens of Nineveh was tied to his ability to wait for God's grace to act freely. It was not about Jonah, and it was not largely about Nineveh. Jonah's situation required a lesson in waiting, because "to wait" was synonymous with "to hope." Jonah misguidedly placed his hope in the work, in his logic about good and evil, and in his ability to serve with integrity as a prophet. What he needed to learn was that all hoping falls on the initiative of an active God, and never on the whim of the penitent.

The Penitential Psalms are never primarily about the penitent, but are always about revealing the nature of God as merciful and forgiving.

"To hope" and "to wait" are repeated throughout this psalm. In Spanish, the word *espero* translates both of these words depending on the context, as does the Hebrew in this psalm. It is the same root word that goes back and forth in meaning—either "to wait" or "to hope" in the Lord. In other words, for the biblical imagination, waiting and hoping are one and the same. "I *hope* for his word," but also, "I *wait* for his word."

This psalm is not based on guilt. The psalmist has found words to define how faith works at a core level. The tension remains in the waiting. I can cry out to God, and I might righteously demand something, or I can provide all the sacrifices I can in order to acquire some response. But none of this would force a response from God, who remains free of my concerns. This is faith. The psalmist has learned to trust in the waiting, and this becomes a source of hope for the word that will come in its time. The psalmist has something to teach the community. "Let Israel wait for the Lord, and he will redeem Israel from all its sins."

The church of the New Testament held onto this psalm as the hallmark of Christian faith. The phrase "I hope for his word" finds its response in the person of Jesus, the Word of the Lord. The reverence owed to God is reverence given to Christ for the disciples that follow him. "But with you is forgiveness and so you are revered." Without waiting for the presence of Christ in our lives, there is no practice of hoping. And if we don't hope, true faith is no longer present. Instead, we might be living out some contractual and distorted version of the faith.

But the presence of God in our lives cannot be commanded or wielded. We can only wait in hope. The extended period of Lent is a time to remember this essential aspect of faith—the act of waiting for the Lord. "My soul looks for the Lord more than sentinels for daybreak. More than sentinels for daybreak."

And in case this truth has yet to sink in, let me repeat it a third time: "More than sentinels for daybreak."

9

Generational Healing

In the morning let me hear of your mercy,
for in you I trust.
Show me the path I should walk,
for I entrust my life to you.

Teach me to do your will,
for you are my God.
May your kind spirit guide me
on ground that is level.

For your name's sake, LORD, give me life;
in your righteousness lead my soul out
of distress.
In your mercy put an end to my foes;
all those who are oppressing my soul,
for I am your servant.

Psalm 143:8, 10–12

The morning is symbolic for surviving the night. Perhaps, the logic goes, in the morning all will be well, all will be forgiven, and I may start fresh again. "The Lord's acts of mercy are not exhausted, his compassion is not spent; they are renewed each morning—great is your faithfulness!" (Lam 3:22–23). The last of the Penitential Psalms begins with lament in form, but ends with the tools for renewal and healing.

Spending time with women in recovery and working through psalms like this one has taught me about generational healing. The older women especially have been to the pit of destruction, and continue to toe the line between sinking back into a past world of pain or continuing to heal. But where could they possibly go? Where could anyone think to go if anyone or anything other than the Spirit is showing the path, teaching and guiding the way?

"Show me the path I should walk, for I entrust my life to you."

Can I say with confidence that I entrust my life to the Creator? The women in recovery are more open and honest about these things than me. They would often tell me exactly how they entrusted their lives to destructive energies. Every one of their misguided decisions stemmed from an ingrained sense of low self-worth. From this ditch they entrusted themselves to all forms of abuse. It's the opposite of that Christmas song where the lyrics ring out, "And the soul felt its worth." In fact, the numbing of the soul is often the only way to limp forward in life.

"For your name's sake, LORD, give me life."

I remember my favorite spiritual exercise I facilitated with a group of powerful women in recovery. We each recalled the earliest religious memory we had growing up. Good or bad, the exercise was meant to tap into those formative childhood experiences. My own earliest memories are on display in the first chapter of this book. They are mostly comforting, and helped set a tone early in my childhood that the church was a safe place. In my imagination the church was a conduit for God's presence in the life of the community. Church always made sense to me. It was a safe space.

But the reflections from these women were varied. Only two had positive experiences of their religious practices from childhood. One participant was filled with anger—the same anger she carried today, but could now recognize and name its source. Another had no memory whatsoever that religion or faith had ever played a role in her life until later, when she started to question the beliefs that guided her path. One woman, who was almost done with her period of rehabilitation at the center, recalled a mixture of her Native faith and Christian belief in Christ as something cohesive, one complementing the other.

All of us, however, were healing and learning from each other in this sacred practice of praying through these early childhood memories. Who am I now? I can clearly see an image of that little kid with big emotions, sometimes stuck in a traumatic environment. But am I the same today? Answering these questions can become a source of healing. They resonate with the last Penitential Psalm: "May your kind spirit guide me on ground that is level." God's kind spirit is always showing the path for those who decide to look up with courage.

The women in recovery faced foes and enemies from every corner. Their main adversaries involved some toxic substance and a false community that fostered abuse rather than healing. They provide a good example for the words of the psalmist: "In your mercy put an end to my foes; all those who are oppressing my soul." But why? The last line of the psalm provides the key to our Lenten pilgrimage and to the purpose of making a spiritual journey: "For I am your servant."

Epilogue

"Everything That Has Breath"

I'm back at it, facilitating soul sessions with the women in recovery on Saturday afternoons. In our last session we focused on the act of breathing. Everyone closed their eyes, slowed down their thoughts, and began to center their breath to a still silence. We reminded ourselves that difficult things require the ability to regulate your breath. Swimming through deep water requires being in sync with your breathing. Running a marathon comes down to breathing. Calming the anxiety of the day is a matter of breathing. Even death is an act of taking one last breath of air before crossing over to the other side. Deep breaths in, and exhaling out all that life offers.

Earlier that same day, I had participated in the last prayers for a woman who passed away on the reservation. She brought together families from three traditions:

Blackfoot, Salish, and Catholic. Her side of the Blackfoot family came forward and shared with the group their Beaver Bundle prayers of encouragement. Their hymn, like a psalm, was performed in mid-pitch range, with short breaths of air in between notes. After the song ended, they explained how the hymn was meant to encourage their sister to make her journey to the other side. They finished with an acknowledgement of their Catholic heritage, especially the prayers she had grown up with and understood. We all prayed, in sync with her Blackfoot family, an Our Father, Hail Mary, and Glory Be. Before the final closing of the casket, the service ended with prayers recited in the Salish language from one of the woman's close friends.

Singing, dying, and praying are all related to breathing.

It does not surprise me that the last psalm from the Bible ends with a hymn of thanksgiving. It does not end with a penitential theme but with perfect praise to the Creator. And the last verse of the last psalm returns to breath: "Let everything that has breath give praise to the LORD" (Ps 150:6). The final recollection is a reminder that everything returns to a breath of gratitude. Lament eventually returns to praise for the author of life. So does hardship, guilt, remorse, failure, and success.

The psalms, especially the Penitential Psalms, bring us down to the pits and back up to level ground again. In the end, the capacity to give praise to God through everything the soul has been through endures as a great sign of biblical wisdom. The good and bad of life are the same at this level of surrender.

"Let everything that has breath give praise to the LORD! Hallelujah!"